Interconnected Threads

Kimberly A. Behan

BookLeaf
Publishing

India | USA | UK

Interconnected Threads © 2023 Kimberly A. Behan

All rights reserved.

Presentation by *BookLeaf Publishing*

Web: www.bookleafpub.com

E-mail: info@bookleafpub.com

ISBN: 9789358314816

First edition 2023

DEDICATION

For my Mom who I always promised I'd dedicate my first book to her. Miss you forever.

ACKNOWLEDGEMENT

Thank you to my husband for giving me space to write these poems this month. I love you.

Thank you to my children for being who you are. I love you both to the moon and back.

PREFACE

I have always wanted to be an author ever since I learned to write. I took on this challenge to write 21 poems in October 2023 and here are the results. If there are any typos, know that editing is not my strong suit in large part due to ADHD. Although I am pretty sure the meaning will still be there.

Interconnected Threads

Weaving the fabric of who I am;
What connects me; who I am
My interconnected threads:
Motherhood.
Pregnancy.
ADHD...late diagnosis [because I am a woman?
Maybe...]
Reader.
Librarian.
Previous single mom turned wife/mother of two.
Picture taker.
Memory maker.
Loss of a brother.
Loss of a mother.
Loss of a birth country, birth family, birth
language—¿Hablas espanol? No, not really.
Threaded throughout these pages
are
these interconnected threads.

Awakening

Awake awake awake
My eyes open to this new role
Of motherhood
in February 2017 when I read
A positive pregnancy test.

My number one dream in the world.
to be a mother
is coming true.
Even though it won't be as ideal as it
could be because I will be a
single mom
But no matter.
I finally will be a mom.
I always felt like I was born
To be a mom
And thanks to this
positive pregnancy test
I am awakening to this new role:
Mom.
I wish I didn't have to mom without my mom

Since she is everything I know about
What it means to be a mom
But there is absolutely

Nothing
I can do to change that fact:
I'll be momming without a mom.

As I awaken to motherhood
Choices are thrust at me:
C-section or "natural" birth
OB GYN or midwives
Hospital birth or homebirth?
To write a birthing plan or not to write one?
Attend birthing classes or not?
Breastfeed or bottle feed?
Co-sleep or crib?
A whole world unfolds before my eyes.
I jump in.

I Hate it Here

The first funeral I can
remember
is my
brother's.
I hate it here.

He was only 32 years old.
Hit and run.
Riding home on his bicycle
Ten years ago.
I hate it here.

Denial denial denial.
I hate it here.

Day arrives for his funeral.
We drove there.
My boyfriend drove I should say
I sit there in numbed silence.
Numbed disbelief.
Pinch self.
Will self to wake up from
Nightmare
Please.
I hate it here.

I feel sick
I feel sad
I feel like I
want
Earth to swallow me whole.
I hate it here.

Standing outside the parking lot
my boyfriend holds my hand.
I'll never be ready to go inside
but I can't stay out there either.
I hate it here.

Cars and cars of people
Arrive.
Everyone in black.
Must join my mom
My dad
My stepmom
To welcome them
To the worst day of my life.
Our lives.
I hate it here.

November chill runs through my
Bones.
Tug of hand.
Feet move forward

Dragging my soul
My heart
Autopilot
Walk through the door.
Walk through the door.
I hate it here.

Can't go in to see my brother
In the casket just yet.
I don't
Have the strength.
Boyfriend holds me up.
A pillar.
Flowers engulf my nostrils.
I gag and have never smelled flowers
the same since.
Flowers smell like death.
Flowers smell like the worst days ever.
I hate it here.

Cousin comes in
Cousin who I haven't seen in ages.
Cousin reprimands me for
Not wearing heels
Since I'm so short
I must be in the Twilight Zone
Because who cares and why care
What is on my feet
Since my brother

lays 50 feet away
in the other room
Never able to wear shoes again.
I hate it here.

More people come in.
My mom is crippled over
Her walker
screaming and crying
Having trouble breathing.
I know I need to go in to comfort her.
Feet autopilot again.
Walk towards her.
Hold her.
My own tears have dried up as if a drought
Has come to my face.
I hate it here.

I walk up to him
laying still
and I need,
no,
want this to be a lie.
My brother can't be dead.
We're supposed to grow old together.
We're not supposed to be here.
One of us alive.
One of us dead.
I hate it here.

Everybody comes out
People I haven't seen in ages
People I haven't thought about in ages
Come to pay their respects
To him
To us
I wish we could have seen these people for
Different reasons.
Different circumstances.
Have I mentioned
I hate it here?

Hands shaken
Hugs given
Tears shed
"He was too young," repeatedly said.
I hate it here.

Priest comes
And I bristle
because my brother wasn't
religious
but
we don't have another way to
do death rituals
and some of our family is religious.
All the same
I hate it here.

Time for eulogies.
I don't know who else speaks
Except for
Mom
Dad
Me.
Parents should never have to
speak at their
child's funeral.
Parents should never have to
bury their children.
It goes against the natural
order of everything.
I hate it here.

November rolls around
Marking his anniversary
Every 18th of the 11th month.
I hate it here.

Focus

ADHD
and my dyscalculia
(yeah there's that too)
make me feel
less of an adult.
I constantly
ask myself
"Am I missing something?"
or
"Am I just stupid?"
Why does 10,000
sound like the same number
as 10,000,000?
Why do I constantly have
3 beverages to drink from?
Why can't I focus?
Why do I only hyper-focus
only on what interests me?
Why wereADHD and dyscalculia missed?
Late to the game at 38 years old.
But at least I am here
and learning
and validating my quirks.
There's more to add
to say

I'm sure
but right on brand...
I can't focus on it right now.

Bittersweet Dream

It was a lovely bittersweet dream
that I wish
didn't end.
In my dream
My brother was
alive again.
He was coming
home
from faraway
for
his birthday.
And to meet
his nephew.
His namesake.
Husband and daughter
weren't there for some reason.
Dad was.
Stepmom was.

Little Chris was being
his silly self.
Goofing off with his Uncle Chris.
We smashed eggs on the floor
for some reason.
It was oddly therapeutic.

Little Chris gave
him a card that said,
"I love you so
I'm giving you my dinosaur."
A drawing of a dinosaur.

I kept taking pictures
because I knew
in the dream
my brother was only visiting for a short time.
I wish
I wish
I wish
those pictures were real.
I checked my phone upon waking knowing they
wouldn't be there
but wishing.

Haiku for my discarded postpartum hair

Postpartum hair loss:
No joke. I could've made a
Blanket with lost hair.

Empty Beach

Empty beach
Just the sounds of waves
I have heard that contractions come in waves…

…And that some people use
that metaphor
of
riding a wave
of a contraction
to help them get to
the end
of one contraction
and to the
next.

I close my eyes and take in the sounds of
the beach
Waves.
Seagulls.
Peace.
This is my happy place.
This is my home.
I touch my
pregnant belly.
This is what I will come home to when I am

in labor.

The beach makes me sleepy and hopeful
that labor will be as easy as
the sea breeze.

I close my eyes and picture
the scene in front of me:
Just me and my baby
With the sun beating down on my skin
And a slight sea breeze just cooling the air
Ever so slightly.
The soft tan sand
The rolling blue waves
And endless sky and ocean
Stretching on forever.

The call of the seagulls.
I know they've been called
"the rats of the sky"
but I find them to be a
quintessential
part
of
the
beach day
experience.

Roller skates

This is about parenting
and grief.
Roller Skates on your feet
Rolling into your 5th birthday
I am
Watching you in your birthday skates
even though it feels like just yesterday
I was in labor with you.
Just yesterday you were learning
to walk.
Now you skate.

Papa and Mimi got you
your birthday skates.

Your dad held your hand
and
my dad tried reaching you
how to skate.
I watched
struck by
how, once long ago,
he was teaching
my brother and me
how to skate.

Suddenly I slip
As if I'm the one
learning to skate
because I feel a
p
 l
  u
   n
    g
     e
of sadness
knowing this is another thing
that was robbed from
your Grandma:
watching you learn to roller skate.
Something simple.
Mostly mundane.
But
she should
be
sitting
in her
wheelchair watching
you roller skate
grinning at you.
Proud of you.
In awe with me
with how much

you've grown.

But no.

Only in my mind
can that happen.

Grandma loves you.

Haiku about Both of my Labors

First labor lasted
forty-seven hours. The
second: twenty . Ugh.

Two Haikus for the Price of One [Wishes]

You grieve because you
loved them so much. I wish they
saw me as a mom.

They always knew I
would be a mom someday; wish
they met my children.

10/11

I have always loved birthdays
So it shouldn't surprise me
how much I love yours.

Your birthday was my first
birthing day.
When you came into this world
I was born
A Mother.

Being your mother
(and of course your sister's mother)
is the best thing that ever happened to me.

Celebrating you is
celebrating all the love in
the world
because
you are
True Love.

The time it takes me to stress over a task (A Haiku)

ADHD is
stressing tasks longer than it
takes to complete them.

A Mother's Love

Motherhood is a contradictory state…
State of mind and being
Being needed all day, everyday, day after day
Day in and day out.
Out of the darkness comes a new life.
Life that rearranges your love.
Love that never will never end.

End of freedom though
Though the beginning of a big transformation.
Transformation that's the biggest.
Biggest, best love and more.
More love, cuddles, and laughter.
Laughter that is the sweetest I ever heard.

Heard your sweet voice for the first time:
Time stood still.
Still I wish Grandma got to meet you.
You remind me of her.
Her soul and eyes.
Eyes being the windows to your soul.
Soul so tiny still but full of life.
Life that I would do anything for.
For you are my child.

Child, I've wished for you since I was a child.
Child, you are everything right in this world.
World so scary I wish I could protect you.
You are my sunshine.
Sunshine that lights me up.

"Up" was one of your first words
Words now spill out of you.
You make new discoveries.
Discoveries lead you to new words.
Words you misspeak or invent.

Invent new worlds and ideas
Ideas that carry us to new places
Places that come from your mind: inherently
good
Good souls like yours breed kind ideas.

Ideas of kindness whirl around,
Around and around now that you're in school.
School can shape who you will become.
Become whatever you want as long as you do it
with kindness
Kindness above everything is what I want to
teach you
You already know kindness
Kindness when you help me around the home.

Home is where you will always find me waiting.

Waiting with open arms.
Arms to embrace and hug
Hug and kisses for you no matter what you do.

Do not be afraid to talk to me about whatever.
Whatever, whenever. Whenever whatever.
Whatever happens you'll always be my child.

Child, I love you to the moon and back.

Stages of Grief

The stages aren't meant
to be applied
to
those
who
were
left behind
in the aftermath of death.
They're there
for those
on their deathbed.

But the stages can still be there
in those
early days especially.

Don't tell me
End this reality
Not this
It must be a lie
Absolutely need them alive
Let it be a lie.

Bring them back
And I'll do anything
Really
Give me my mom and brother back
And
I'll
Never
Imagine again
Not being the best person I can be
Given the circumstances.

Anger is everywhere
Nowhere is safe
Going crazy with these angry thoughts
Every day
Raining on my heart.

Depression is a shadow that follows me
Everywhere
Please fuck off.
Really don't need more depression
Every damn day
Slithering
Sulking
In every
Occasion
Now and forever.

As if I
Could ever accept their deaths
Considering
Everything about their deaths.
Please.
That can't
And won't ever
Never happen.
Can't live without them.
Ever.

ADHD Always

Scattered scrolling
Dopamine drip
'Nother notification
ADHD always.

Forced focus
Distinct determination
Pivot, pull
ADHD always.

Mindless musings
Social media : sucking minds
Stay sharp.
ADHD always.

Don't dare
to tempt
increased interest
ADHD always.

Threading takes
Sewing samples
Yielding yarn
ADHD always.

Elsewhere enticing
Stop scrolling
Create content [content creation]
ADHD always.

5:53 PM // No Words

Writing time
Walking around
in circles
Downtown Brooklyn
October 16th
5:53 PM
And I notice
A man wearing
a tan backpack.
Some Spanish words
and the word:
Colombia.

And I have
two thoughts
simultaneously:
-Colombia, you are filled with contradictions
and conflicting feelings for me
-It's time to
write more
about adoption.

I am an adoptee
from Colombia.

Although adoptee
isn't the
right word
really.

There actually
isn't a word
for what I am.

At least not just
one word.

Yes.
Adoptee
in theory.
But

What is the word

For someone

Stolen at birth?

What is the word
for
having the language
you should be speaking
&
writing in

stolen from you?

What is the word
for
feeling
guilty and glad
that you
were
stolen?
Because this life
here in
America
is the one
you
are
grateful
to have.

There is no word.

Hug Haiku for CRM

35

Your hug is the best.
Your hug is the answer to
the world's problems.

A decade

In one month
from today
it will be
10 years...
[a decade]
since your passing.

10 years.
It feels like
yesterday.
It feels like
a lifetime ago.

Sometimes
I wonder:
"Did I make you up?"
"Did I really have a brother?"
Picture proves positive
luckily.
A decade.

3,652 days
have passed
with
all these significant

events
that it doesn't seem
real
that
you
weren't here for
like:
My break-up with the last boyfriend who knew
you
Going back to school to be a librarian
Our niece being born
Mom passing away
My pregnancy and birth with your namesake
My first job as a librarian
Covid-19/pandemic/quarantine
Falling in love with my
now husband
Most of Dad's 2nd marriage
The amazing person our stepmom is
Our step-siblings passing away
The pregnancy and birth of your niece.

A decade…
that you should've
been part of…

When I Think About Colombia

I sometimes
think
about what life
could've been
had
I not
been
stolen
at birth...

Because
I am
always
feeling
guiltily grateful
that
I was
and
I wonder:
Is that
just because
this is
the only
life I

know?

When I think
about Colombia,
it all feels...
[too]
complicated.

My kid's #1 enemy

The enemy is
safety torture device: a
car seat: children's hell.

In the end

In the end, here are all these words,
words that make up my life.
Life that was stolen.
Stolen but grateful.
Grateful and guilty.
Guilty to have all of this.

This is my world and all I know.
Know that
that will never really change.

Change happens though
Though not as expected always.

Always grateful for the next adventure.
Adventure that comes as the threads
thread and weave together.

Together making my life one that is lived.